Licensed exclusively to Top That Publishing Ltd
Tide Mill Way, Woodbridge, Suffolk, IP12 1AP, UK
www.topthatpublishing.com
Copyright © 2014 Tide Mill Media
All rights reserved
2 4 6 8 9 7 5 3 1
Printed and bound in China

ISBN 978-1-78244-953-9

A catalogue record for this book is available from the British Library

VALLEY OF THE DINOSAURS

Millions of years ago, long before humans existed,
Earth belonged to the dinosaurs.

Herds of plant-eating dinosaurs roamed across the land where fierce, meat-eating predators hunted and pterosaurs ruled the skies.

There wasn't any grass when dinosaurs roamed Earth. Instead, the land was covered in a blanket of conifers and ferns.

At the end of the dinosaurs' time on Earth, early
flowers and trees such as oak, beech, walnut
and maple started to appear.

Can you spot the dinosaurs who are hiding
amongst the prehistoric plants and trees?

It's time to meet the dinosaurs who live in the valley ...

There is no mistaking plant-eating Triceratops with three huge horns sticking out of its head and a colourful bony frill around its neck!

Triceratops lived in large herds and used their bony neck frills and horns to defend themselves against predators like Tyrannosaurus rex.

Slow-moving Stegosaurus had large bony plates running along its back and a spiked tail, which it used to defend itself.

Despite being nearly nine metres long, plant-eating Stegosaurus had a very small brain, which was about the size of a kiwi fruit!

Weighing around 8 tonnes and at 12 metres long, Tyrannosaurus rex was one of the most deadly dinosaur predators of all time!

Tyrannosaurus rex had a large head
with powerful jaws and dagger-like teeth.
It could run very fast over short distances.

Brachiosaurus had an enormous neck that enabled it to eat the fresh fruit and leaves growing high off the ground.

This slow-moving dinosaur giant needed to feed from morning until night just to stay alive. It grew up to 26 metres in length and weighed around 35 tonnes!

Pteranodons ruled the skies at the time of the dinosaurs and used their two-metre-long wings to fly far out to sea in order to hunt for fish.

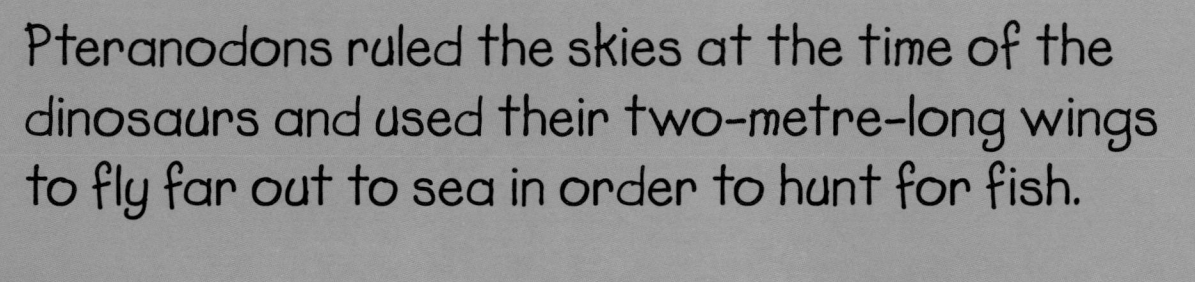

The Pteranodons' wings were so large in comparison to their feet, that they probably had to launch off cliffs in order to take off.

Before they became extinct (died out), there were hundreds of different types of dinosaur. Do you recognise any of the dinosaurs who are roaming through Dino Valley?